100 Things
you should know about
Rocks & Minerals

100 Things
you should know about
Rocks &
Minerals

Sean Callery

Consultant: Steve Parker

MASON CREST PUBLISHERS INC.
370 Reed Road
Broomall, Pennsylvania 19008
(866)MCP-BOOK (toll free)
www.masoncrest.com

ISBN: 978-1-4222-2005-4
Series ISBN (15 titles): 978-1-4222-1993-5

First Printing
9 8 7 6 5 4 3 2 1

Cataloging-in-Publication Data on file with the Library of Congress.
Printed in the U.S.A.

First published in 2009 by Miles Kelly Publishing Ltd
Bardfield Centre, Great Bardfield, Essex, CM7 4SL

Editorial Director: Belinda Gallagher

Art Director: Jo Brewer

Senior Editor: Rosie McGuire

Editorial Assistant: Claire Philip

Volume Designer: Andrea Slane

Image Manager: Lorraine King

Indexer: Jane Parker

Production Manager: Elizabeth Brunwin

Reprographics: Anthony Cambray, Stephan Davis

Archive Manager: Jennifer Hunt

ACKNOWLEDGEMENTS
The publishers would like to thank the following artists
who have contributed to this book:

Mike Foster, Mike Saunders

All other artworks are from the Miles Kelly Artwork Bank

The publishers would like to thank the following sources for the use of their photographs:
Cover Adam Jones/Science Photo Library;
Page 6 Michael Krabs/Imagebroker/FLPA; 10–11 Jim Sugar/Corbis; 11 Micha Pawlitzki/zefa/Corbis;
12(t) Roger Ressmeyer/Corbis; 13(t) Reuters/Corbis; 14–15 Tim Fitzharris/Minden Pictures/FLPA;
17 David Muench/Corbis; 18 nagelstock.com/Alamy; 19 Frank Lukasseck/Corbis; 21 Ric Ergenbright/Corbis;
22 Tony and Daphne Hallas/Science Photo Library; 22 Richard Bizley/Science Photo Library;
23 NASA Kennedy Space Center; 26 Tim Fitzharris/Minden Pictures/FLPA; 27 Paul A. Souders/Corbis;
28(t) Cornelius/Fotolia; 29 Stephen Barnett/Photolibrary; 30 Javier Trueba/MSF/Science Photo Library;
32(t) Domen Colja/Fotolia, (cl) Graça Victoria/Fotolia; 34 Ria Novosti/Science Photo Library; 35(t) sharply_done/Fotolia,
(bl) Mark huls/Fotolia, (r) Bruno Bernier/Fotolia; 36 Michael Yamashita/Corbis; 37 Trent Warner/Rex Features;
38(t) Andreas Meyer/Fotolia, (br) Jean-Claude Revy, ISM/Science Photo Library; 39(t) Jim Pickerell/Photolibrary,
(inset) A Marcynuk/Fotolia, (br) Jason Hawkes/Corbis; 40 Anthony Bannister; Gallo Images/Corbis;
41(t, l–r) NiDerLander/Fotolia, Maksim Shebeko/Fotolia, (tr) Darren Hester/Fotolia; 42–43(bg) martreya/Forolia;
42–43(t) Getty Images; 44(t) Anthony Bannister, Gallo Images/Corbis, (br) Rex Features;
45(t) Prudence Cuming/ScienceLtd/WhiteCube/Rex Features, (b) Bettmann/Corbis;
46 George Steinmetz/Corbis; 47(t) Roger Ressmeyer/Corbis; (b)Corbis

All other photographs are from:

Corel, digitalSTOCK, digitalvision, iStockphoto.com, John Foxx, PhotoAlto,
PhotoDisc, PhotoEssentials, PhotoPro, Stockbyte

Contents

All around us

1 **Rocks and minerals form our planet, so they are all around us.** Minerals are the building blocks of rocks. They are formed inorganically, meaning no living thing helps to create them. Rocks are aggregates (combinations) of particles from one or more minerals. Rocks and minerals make up much of the Earth and we couldn't live without them. We use them for building, cleaning, art —we even eat them.

▲ The Marble Cathedral or grotto (cave), under Lake General Carrera, on the borders of Chile and Patagonia. The marble was formed by intense heat from other kinds of rocks and then worn away (eroded) into these beautiful shapes by the constant movement of the water.

The rock cycle

2 **There are layers inside the Earth.** The first is the crust (the solid outer shell), which is between 4 and 43 miles (6 and 70 kilometers) thick. Under this is the mantle—a layer of hot rock that is around 1,550 miles (2,500 kilometers) thick. The uppermost layers of the mantle are fused to the crust. Beneath these layers is an outer core of liquid metal and an inner core—a solid ball of hot iron.

Inner core

Outer core

Mantle

Crust

▲ Under the crust and mantle are layers of liquid metal and, in the center, a solid ball of sizzling iron.

Weathering of rocks at surface

► The rock cycle is the long, slow journey of rocks down from the surface and then up again. Rocks are often changed during this process.

Erosion and transport

Laying down of sediment

3 **All rock goes through a cycle over millions of years.** During the rock cycle, rocks form deep in the Earth, move and sometimes change, go up to the surface and eventually return below the ground. There are three kinds of rock—igneous, sedimentary and metamorphic. They form in different ways and have different features.

Burial and becoming more compact under pressure

SEDIMENTARY ROCK

Deep burial and metamorphism (changing

4 Rocks can go around the cycle in lots of ways. Igneous rocks were once molten (liquid), and have hardened beneath or above the surface. Metamorphic rock forms when rock is changed by heat, pressure or a combination of the two. Sedimentary rocks are formed when sediment— small particles of rock—becomes buried.

5 Exposed rock is eroded (worn away) over time. This is a process in which tiny pieces (particles) of rock are loosened and transported as a result of gravity, wind, water or ice. Gradually these particles may become buried under more rock particles, forming sediment. If the sediment is buried deep enough to reach the mantle it will be heated by magma (hot molten rock), which may melt or bake it. Uplift and erosion can then expose them again.

IGNEOUS ROCK

Magma forms crystals as it cools

METAMORPHIC ROCK

Melting to form magma

Formed in fire

6 Rock that forms when hot molten rock (magma or lava) cools and hardens is called **igneous rock.** Igneous rock is divided into two types, extrusive and intrusive, depending on where it forms.

◀ When the pressure in the magma chamber is high enough, the volcano erupts and spews out its lava with incredible force.

7 **Igneous rock is known as "extrusive" if it forms above Earth's surface.** This can happen if it erupts or flows from a volcano as lava. Sometimes lava settles, sealing the volcano until pressure builds for another eruption. Extrusive rock can form over thousands or even millions of years. As extrusive rock cools, its fine grains grow into larger crystals.

8 **Intrusive rock cools and solidifies inside the Earth's crust, below the surface.** It only becomes visible when the rocks above it wear away. Granite and dolerite are two examples of intrusive rock.

▶ An ancient volcanic eruption formed the Giant's Causeway, which consists of around 40,000 columns of basalt that interlock like a giant jigsaw.

9 **The most common type of igneous rock is basalt, which often cools in hexagonal columns.** At the Giant's Causeway in Northern Ireland, thousands of these columns were created as lava cooled and shrank over millions of years. Legend says that the columns, some as much as 7 feet (2 meters) in height, are stepping stones for giants to walk across the sea.

10 **Sometimes gas creates holes in rock.** Crystals form inside the holes, creating geodes — dull-looking stones from the outside, lined with brilliant crystals on the inside. Geodes are often sold cut in half and polished to reveal their glittering insides.

▶ Geodes are rock cavities with crystal formations or circular bands inside them.

▼ Volcanic ash settled over the dead of Pompeii. Over time, the bodies rotted away leaving cavities in the ash. The scientists who uncovered these filled them with plaster to create casts of the victims' bodies.

11 The igneous rock basalt is so durable that it was used to pave the ancient Roman city of **Pompeii.** However, in 79 CE the nearby volcano Vesuvius erupted, covering the town with fresh ash. Buildings, streets and many people were buried and lay untouched for centuries.

▼ Pumice is frothy lava turned solid. It is widely used to make lightweight concrete.

12 **Pumice is solidified lava.** It is so light it will float until water soaks into it. It has tiny holes with sharp edges all over it, making it ideal for rubbing down rough surfaces and cleaning skin. Stonewashed jeans are treated with ground-up pumice.

13 **Granite has a high content of the mineral quartz.** This makes it very tough, so it is often used for construction. It can be seen in many famous buildings, such as parts of London's Tower Bridge and some of the ancient Egyptian pyramids and obelisks.

▲ Curling is an event at the Winter Olympics. Teams slide granite stones toward a target.

14 **The sport of curling uses granite stones.** Teams slide large, heavy, polished granite discs along ice toward a target. Two sweepers with brooms brush the ice to make the stone go in the direction that they want.

◀ Ancient Egyptian obelisks such as this have survived for thousands of years because granite is so tough it takes ages to erode.

15 **Igneous rock is crushed to make aggregate.** This is the material used for the foundations of roads and railways. It forms a strong, stable base on top of which the road surface can be laid. You can sometimes see it as the layer underneath the road surface when roads are being repaired.

16 When rocks are weathered or eroded, they break into tiny pieces called sediment. This sediment is eventually buried and compacted (packed tightly together) under pressure until it becomes solid, forming sedimentary rock. It is found in layers known as strata.

17 The walls of the Grand Canyon in Arizona are sedimentary rock. The canyon is 217 miles (350 kilometers) long and has a depth of one mile (1.6 kilometers) in places. It was created by the flowing force of the Colorado River, which wore away the rock. Rock layers are clearly visible along the sides of the canyon.

18 Limestone is a sedimentary rock mostly formed from crushed shells. It contains the remains of millions of sea creatures that have piled up over millions of years, and so it often contains fossils.

I DON'T BELIEVE IT!

Uluru in Australia is the most famous block of freestanding rock. It is a 1,142-foot-high (348-meter-high) lump of sandstone and is 300 million years old.

19 **Some sedimentary rocks are formed when saline (salt) water evaporates.** This can happen when a bay or gulf is cut off from the sea and starts to dry up. These mineral-rich rocks are known as evaporites and include gypsum, rock salt (halite) and potash.

20 **Coal is a sedimentary rock formed over millions of years.** Vegetation from swampy forests died and rotted away. As the water dried out, the vegetation became first peat and eventually coal. Both peat and coal can be mined and burned as fuel.

◄ The Grand Canyon was formed by two billion years of erosion from the Colorado River exposing countless layers of sedimentary rock.

Super sedimentary

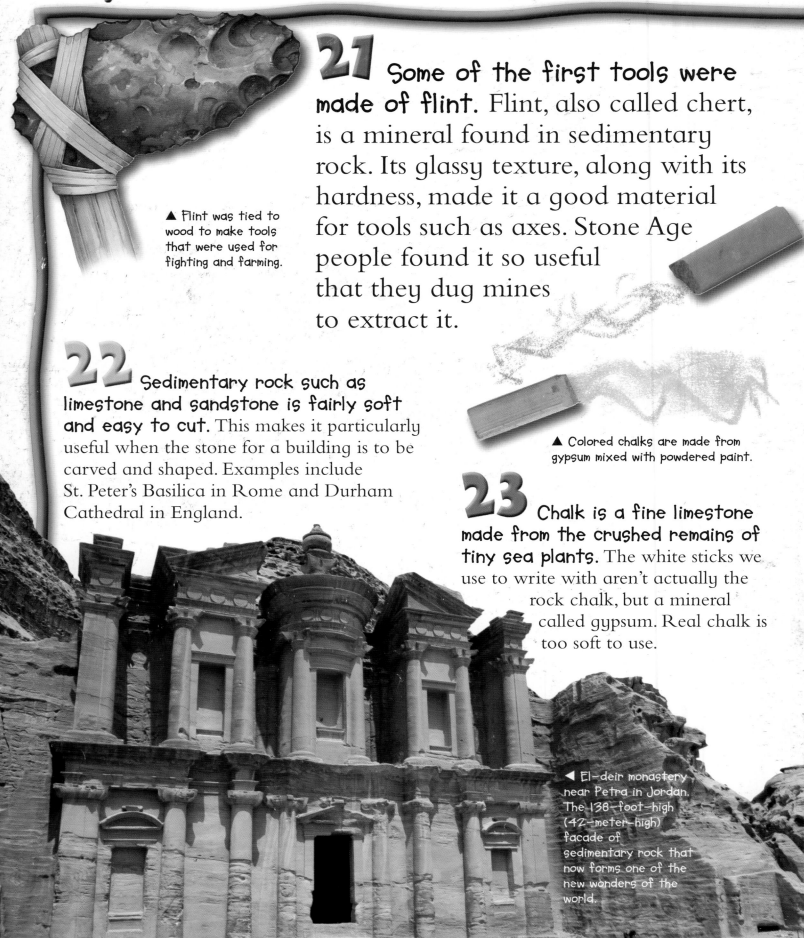

21 **Some of the first tools were made of flint.** Flint, also called chert, is a mineral found in sedimentary rock. Its glassy texture, along with its hardness, made it a good material for tools such as axes. Stone Age people found it so useful that they dug mines to extract it.

▲ Flint was tied to wood to make tools that were used for fighting and farming.

▲ Colored chalks are made from gypsum mixed with powdered paint.

22 **Sedimentary rock such as limestone and sandstone is fairly soft and easy to cut.** This makes it particularly useful when the stone for a building is to be carved and shaped. Examples include St. Peter's Basilica in Rome and Durham Cathedral in England.

23 **Chalk is a fine limestone made from the crushed remains of tiny sea plants.** The white sticks we use to write with aren't actually the rock chalk, but a mineral called gypsum. Real chalk is too soft to use.

◄ El-deir monastery near Petra in Jordan. The 138-foot-high (42-meter-high) facade of sedimentary rock that now forms one of the new wonders of the world.

Make sure you ask an adult to help you. Dissolve some Epsom salts (magnesium sulphate) in two jars of hot water. Drape string between the two jars with each end in the liquid, holding it in place with a paper clip. Leave for a few days and a stalactite should start to form on the string.

24 Stalactites are an amazing feature of some limestone caves. A stalactite develops when a drop of water evaporates, leaving behind a mineral deposit of calcite. If this keeps happening, a spike of mineral starts to "grow" as more water drips down. Stalactites only grow a few fractions of an inch a year.

▼ Stalactites are formed by slow dripping water, just like icicles, except the water has evaporated, leaving its minerals behind. The shapes made when stalactites and stalagmites join into pillars have been called "organ pipes" and "hanging curtains."

25 Sometimes the minerals falling from a stalactite collect on the cave floor and start to "grow" up, making a stalagmite. Eventually the two might meet and join, forming a column. A good way to remember the difference between stalactites and stalagmites is: Watch out! If stalactites grow down, stalag*mites might* grow up.

The rock that changes

26 Metamorphic rock is rock that has been changed by heat or pressure (or both) into a new form deep underground. Pressure from movement of the Earth's crust, the weight of the rocks above and heat from magma cause metamorphic changes. Most of these happen at temperatures of 392°–932° F (200°–500° C). The rock does not melt—that would make igneous rock—but it is altered.

▼ Part of a slate landscape on Valencia Island off the coast of Ireland. This useful rock has been quarried and mined for thousands of years.

27 The appearance and texture of rock changes as a result of heat and pressure. Crystals break down and form, and a rock's chemical structure can change as its minerals react together. If the change is made under pressure, the rock crystals grow flat and form layers. If shale is compressed it forms slate.

▼ Slate forms when fine clay settles in layers and is then compressed and heated.

1. Bands of shale form solid layers

Shale

2. Movement creates curves

Slate

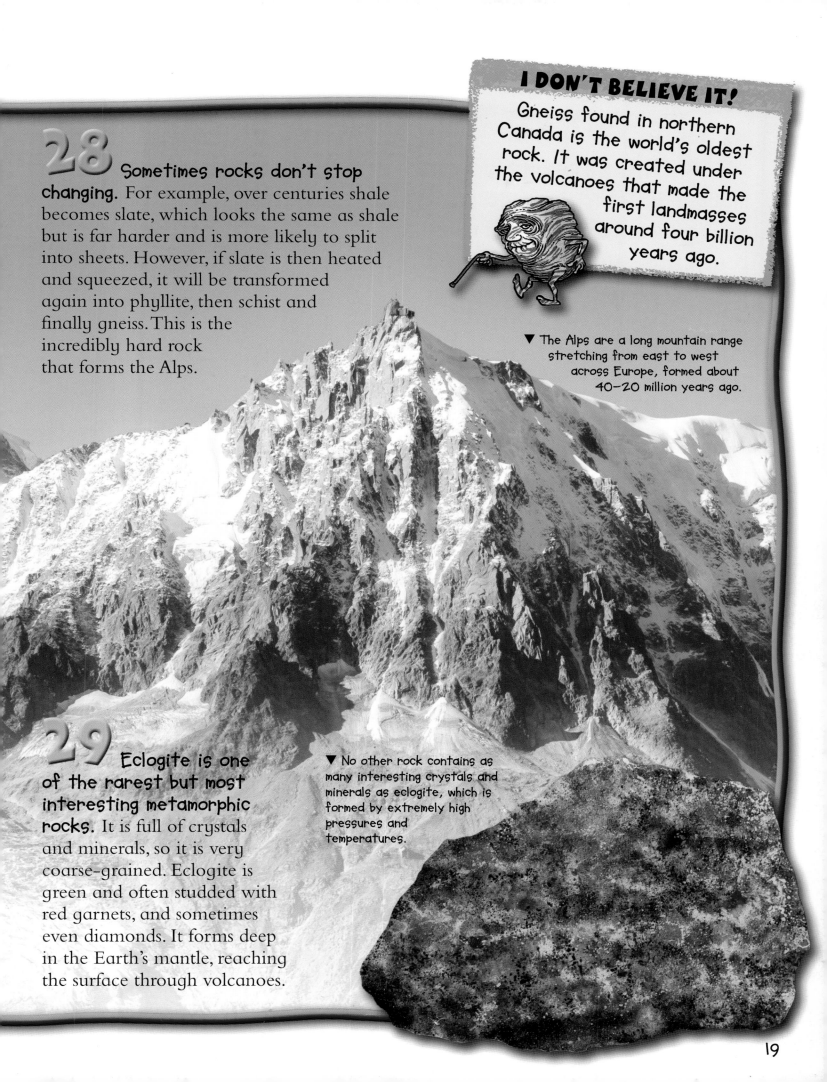

28 Sometimes rocks don't stop changing. For example, over centuries shale becomes slate, which looks the same as shale but is far harder and is more likely to split into sheets. However, if slate is then heated and squeezed, it will be transformed again into phyllite, then schist and finally gneiss. This is the incredibly hard rock that forms the Alps.

▼ The Alps are a long mountain range stretching from east to west across Europe, formed about 40–20 million years ago.

29 Eclogite is one of the rarest but most interesting metamorphic rocks. It is full of crystals and minerals, so it is very coarse-grained. Eclogite is green and often studded with red garnets, and sometimes even diamonds. It forms deep in the Earth's mantle, reaching the surface through volcanoes.

▼ No other rock contains as many interesting crystals and minerals as eclogite, which is formed by extremely high pressures and temperatures.

Marvelous metamorphic

30 The metamorphic rock marble is used in building. It is especially good for curved buildings, such as the Taj Mahal in India. The dome is made of white marble and seems to change color through the day. It took 20,000 workers 22 years to finish the temple and the surrounding buildings in 1648.

▼ The Taj Mahal is an intricately carved, symmetrical tomb made of white marble. It is now a World Heritage Site.

▼ Marble can be cut in any direction and has been used by artists for thousands of years.

31 Marble was a favorite material of Greek and Roman sculptors. Pure marble only contains one mineral—calcite—so it is not formed in bands. This means it is smooth and can be easily carved, so it is perfect for creating complex shapes. The best-known marble comes from Italy.

32 Some Inuit people of the Arctic carve sculptures using the metamorphic rock serpentinite. It has the dark greens, browns and blacks of snakeskin, which is how it got its name (serpent means snake).

▼ The Inuit travel for days to reach supplies of serpentinite, which they carve into beautiful shapes such as this bird.

▼ Slate is light, hard and easy to shape, so it is an ideal material for roofing tiles, where its colors add to the beauty of the building.

33 Slate is a very different kind of metamorphic rock. It is light but hard, water-resistant and can be split into thin sheets, so it is an ideal material for roofing tiles. It is also used to make smooth, flat bases for pool tables.

Space rocks

34 Meteoroids, asteroids and comets are all rocky objects flying through space. Around 1,000 meteoroids, which are the smallest types, land on Earth each year as meteorites. The largest meteorite fell onto Namibia, Africa, around 80,000 years ago. Known as the Hoba meteorite, it is thought to weigh over 60 tons and is the biggest naturally-made piece of iron on Earth's surface.

▶ The moon's surface is covered with craters blasted out by asteroids and comets. The craters are preserved by the lack of atmosphere.

35 Some meteorites have smashed huge craters in the Earth. One rock that hit Vredefort, South Africa, is estimated to be more than 6 miles (10 kilometers) wide and blasted a crater 155 miles (250 kilometers) across. Another, at Meteor Crater in Arizona, blasted out 175 million tons of rock in an explosion about 150 times as powerful as the atomic bombs dropped on Japan during World War II.

36 Small grains of space rock can burn up upon entering Earth's atmosphere. When this happens, they look like streaks of light flying through the night sky. Meteoroids heading toward Earth heat up and some turn into balls of fire. We call these shooting stars. The lumps of rock that land on the Earth are called meteorites. More than 30,000 have been found.

◀ Comets leave a trail of dust and ice. If these fragments reach Earth, they burn up and we see them as jets of light shooting across the sky.

37 **Tests on rocks from the moon show the oldest date back 4.5 billion years.** The most ancient rocks on Earth are younger, at 4 billion years. We can study lunar rock because it has been collected by space missions and some small amounts have fallen to Earth as meteorites. All moon rock is igneous.

▶ The six Apollo moon–landing missions collected 2,415 samples of Moon rock. It has high levels of a mineral called anorthite.

I DON'T BELIEVE IT!

Some scientists believe the dinosaurs were wiped out by a meteorite fall that threw up so much dust it blocked out the sun and changed the climate.

Time capsules

38 Fossils are time capsules buried in rock. They form when a dead animal or plant is buried in sediment, which slowly turns into rock. Sometimes the plant or animal dissolves, leaving a gap of the same shape. This gap is then filled by minerals that create a perfect replica in the mold.

39 More animals have become extinct (died out) than are living today, and we only know about them from fossils. For example, no one has ever seen a living dinosaur, but through fossils we have learned about the many types of these reptiles that ruled the Earth for 175 million years.

▼ Only a tiny number of animals and plants have been fossilized, because the conditions have to be just right.

1. The animal dies and its soft parts rot or are eaten

2. It is covered by sediment, slowing its decay

3. More layers form, and the skeleton is replaced by minerals

4. The upper rocks wear away, and the fossil is exposed

I DON'T BELIEVE IT!

Not all fossils are stone. Tree sap hardens into amber, and sometimes insects and tiny animals become trapped in sap. When the sap hardens, the animal is preserved inside the amber forever.

40 The study of fossils is called paleontology. One of its first experts was Georges Cuvier (1769–1832). He could work out what a prehistoric animal looked like from studying its fossils and comparing them with the anatomies of living animals, and proved that there were animals alive in the past that are now extinct.

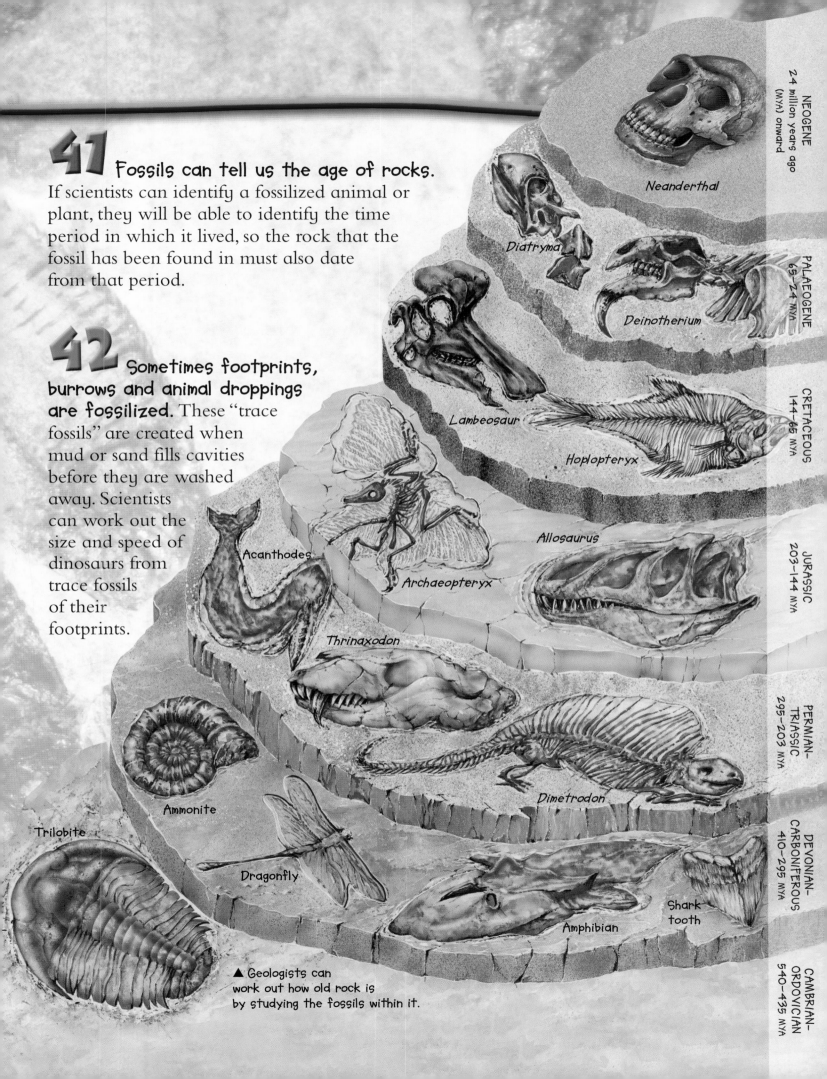

41 Fossils can tell us the age of rocks.
If scientists can identify a fossilized animal or
plant, they will be able to identify the time
period in which it lived, so the rock that the
fossil has been found in must also date
from that period.

42 Sometimes footprints,
burrows and animal droppings
are fossilized. These "trace
fossils" are created when
mud or sand fills cavities
before they are washed
away. Scientists
can work out the
size and speed of
dinosaurs from
trace fossils
of their
footprints.

Neanderthal

Diatryma

Deinotherium

Lambeosaur

Hoplopteryx

Allosaurus

Archaeopteryx

Acanthodes

Thrinaxodon

Dimetrodon

Ammonite

Dragonfly

Trilobite

Amphibian

Shark
tooth

▲ Geologists can
work out how old rock is
by studying the fossils within it.

NEOGENE
24 million years ago
(MYA) onward

PALAEOGENE
65–24 MYA

CRETACEOUS
144–65 MYA

JURASSIC
203–144 MYA

PERMIAN–
TRIASSIC
295–203 MYA

DEVONIAN–
CARBONIFEROUS
410–295 MYA

CAMBRIAN–
ORDOVICIAN
540–435 MYA

The changing landscape

43 **Rocks form our landscape, but they are slowly changing all the time.** They are always being pulled down by gravity, but rocks can also be pushed up from below or worn down in different ways. Many things affect how fast rock is broken down, but it happens to all exposed rock eventually.

44 **When movement wears down rocks, it is known as erosion.** This might be a pebble being ground down as it rolls down a river or glacier, or the top of a hill on a scenic spot being pounded by the feet of countless visitors.

45 **When rocks break down without moving it is known as weathering.** This can be because of rain, frost, sun or wind. Flowing water wears rock away, which is often how valleys form. If the water falls inside a crack and then freezes and expands, it can shatter the rock. This is called frost damage.

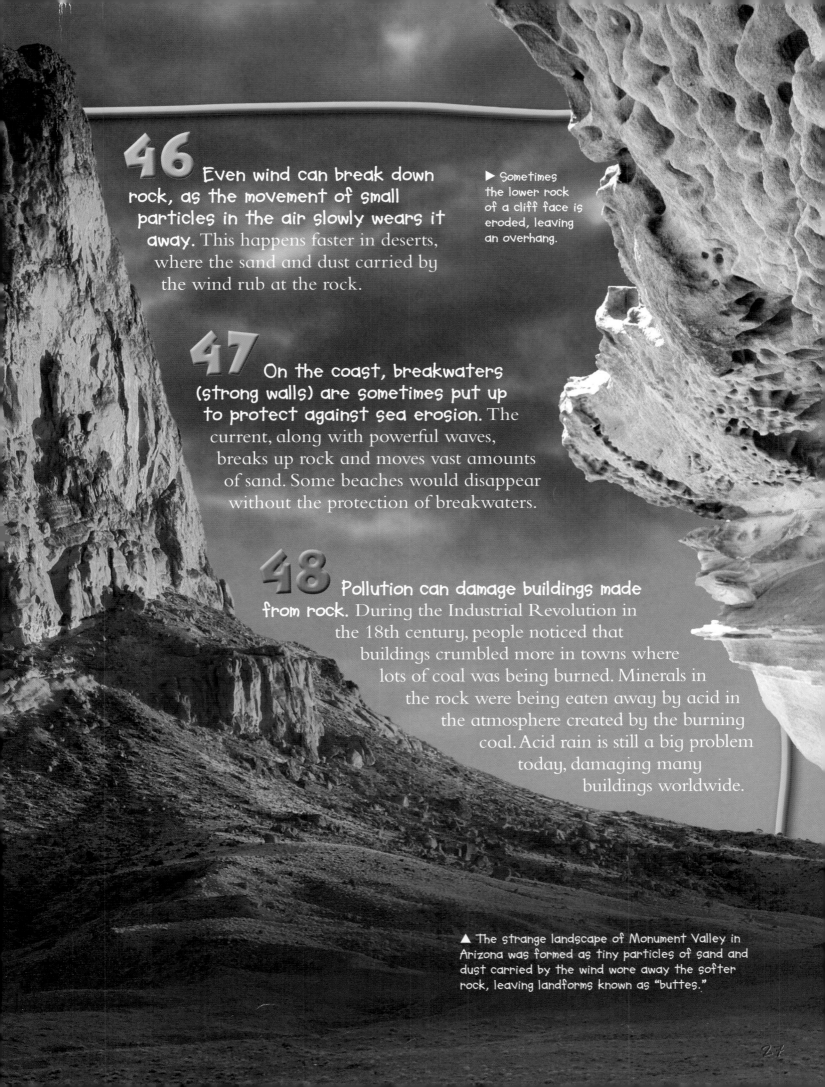

46 Even wind can break down rock, as the movement of small particles in the air slowly wears it away. This happens faster in deserts, where the sand and dust carried by the wind rub at the rock.

▶ Sometimes the lower rock of a cliff face is eroded, leaving an overhang.

47 On the coast, breakwaters (strong walls) are sometimes put up to protect against sea erosion. The current, along with powerful waves, breaks up rock and moves vast amounts of sand. Some beaches would disappear without the protection of breakwaters.

48 Pollution can damage buildings made from rock. During the Industrial Revolution in the 18th century, people noticed that buildings crumbled more in towns where lots of coal was being burned. Minerals in the rock were being eaten away by acid in the atmosphere created by the burning coal. Acid rain is still a big problem today, damaging many buildings worldwide.

▲ The strange landscape of Monument Valley in Arizona was formed as tiny particles of sand and dust carried by the wind wore away the softer rock, leaving landforms known as "buttes."

What are minerals?

49 **Minerals are natural substances that form crystals.** There are over 4,000 different minerals, but only about 30 are found all over the world. Quartz and feldspar are two of the most common types of mineral.

Cubic

▼ Crystal shapes are set by the arrangement of atoms and molecules inside the mineral.

Tetragonal

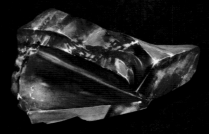
Orthorhombic

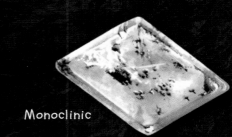
Monoclinic

50 **A mineral is a chemical compound (a combination of two or more substances) or element (a single fundamental substance).** Rocks are made from minerals. Limestone is made mainly of the mineral calcite (calcium carbonate), and granite contains quartz, mica and feldspar.

Triclinic

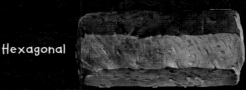
Hexagonal

Trigonal

51 **Minerals form crystals.** They can do this in several ways. Some are formed as hot molten magma cools. Others come from water (the white powder left when water evaporates is a mineral deposit). Crystals can also be formed when minerals are altered by heat or pressure.

52 **Crystals have seven basic shapes.** Some just look like a jumble of different surfaces and angles. They have flat, often shiny, faces and sharp edges.

53 **The tiny grains you can see in most rocks are actually minerals, often forced together.** Large crystals form in cracks and holes in rocks, where they have space to grow. The deeper the rock, the longer it generally takes to reach the surface, and the more time the crystal has to grow.

► Miners have to follow the direction of the mineral-rich band in the seam of rock.

54 **Some minerals are so valuable that they are mined.** This might mean scraping them from the ground, or blowing up the rocks that hold them. Minerals buried deep underground are reached by drilling down and digging tunnels. People have mined minerals for thousands of years.

Mineral detectives

55 **Minerals can be tricky to identify.** Mineralogists (scientists who study minerals) use a number of tests to identify minerals. These are crystal shape, color, streak, magnetism, density, how it splits, and how it reacts to acid.

56 **The same mineral can be different colors, so it can be more helpful for mineralogists to assess how well a mineral reflects light.** This is known as luster. It might shine like metal (metallic), or glisten like glass (vitreous), or be transparent, or block light (opaque).

▲ These giant selenite crystals are believed to be the biggest crystals in the world.

▼ These long, thin crystals belong to a mineral called stibnite.

57 **Another way to identify a mineral is to test how easy it is to scratch.** Minerals are given a "hardness" rating from 1 to 10. If a mineral can be scratched with a fingernail, its hardness is less than 2.5. If it can be scratched with a bronze coin, it has a hardness of 4. If it can be scratched with a pocketknife, it has a hardness 6. The softest mineral, with a score of 1, is talc. Diamonds score 10, because only other diamonds can cut them.

▼ The hardness scale was devised in 1812 by Friedrich Mohs and is still used today.

①	②	③	④
Talc	Gypsum	Calcite	Fluorite

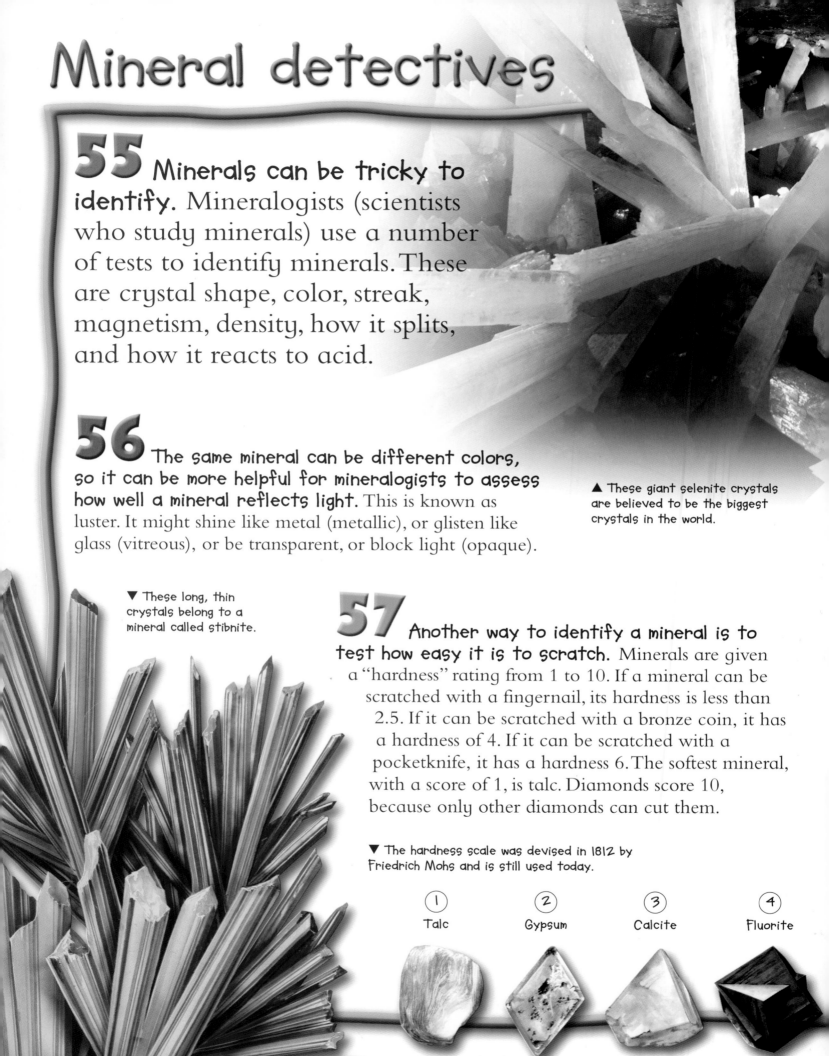

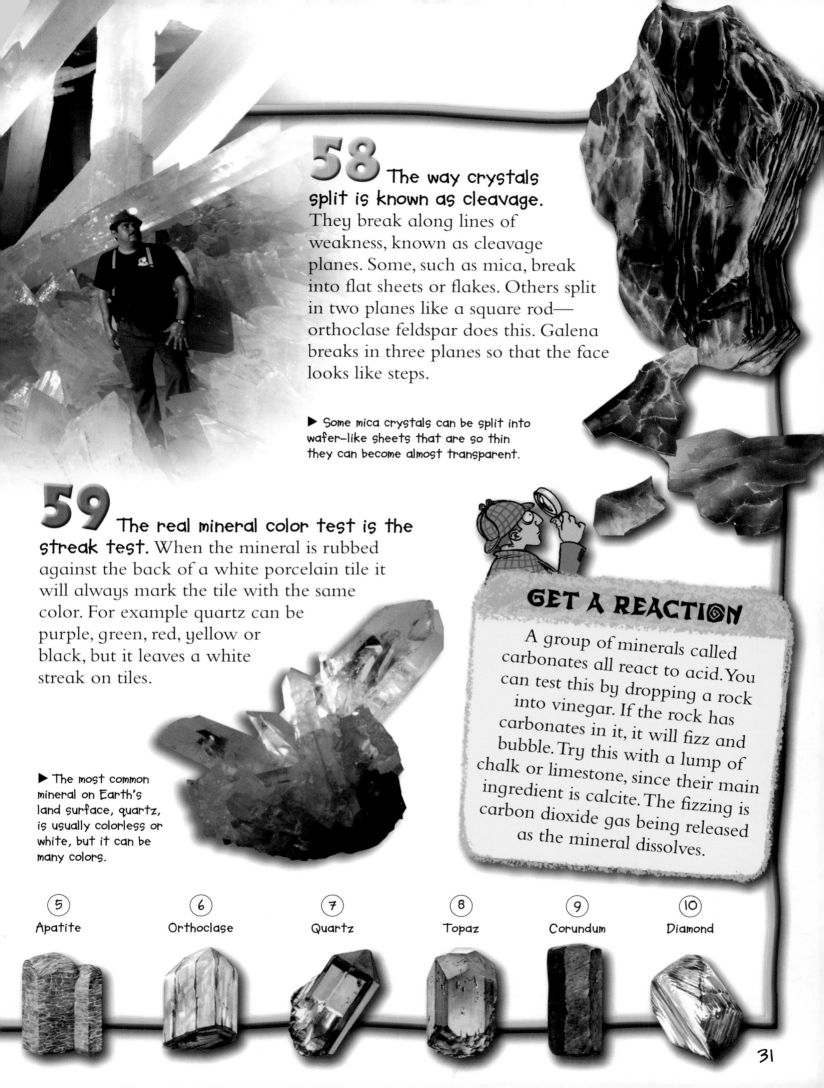

58 The way crystals split is known as cleavage. They break along lines of weakness, known as cleavage planes. Some, such as mica, break into flat sheets or flakes. Others split in two planes like a square rod—orthoclase feldspar does this. Galena breaks in three planes so that the face looks like steps.

▶ Some mica crystals can be split into wafer-like sheets that are so thin they can become almost transparent.

59 The real mineral color test is the streak test. When the mineral is rubbed against the back of a white porcelain tile it will always mark the tile with the same color. For example quartz can be purple, green, red, yellow or black, but it leaves a white streak on tiles.

▶ The most common mineral on Earth's land surface, quartz, is usually colorless or white, but it can be many colors.

GET A REACTION

A group of minerals called carbonates all react to acid. You can test this by dropping a rock into vinegar. If the rock has carbonates in it, it will fizz and bubble. Try this with a lump of chalk or limestone, since their main ingredient is calcite. The fizzing is carbon dioxide gas being released as the mineral dissolves.

(5)	(6)	(7)	(8)	(9)	(10)
Apatite	Orthoclase	Quartz	Topaz	Corundum	Diamond

Brilliant colors

60 The caves of Lascaux in France are decorated with nearly 2,000 figures painted onto the walls by cave dwellers nearly 17,000 years ago. They painted horses, stags, bison and huge bulls using ground-down minerals.

◀ Charcoal is just burnt wood, so there was a plenty of it around for Stone Age artists.

61 Minerals were used for thousands of years to make pigments. At first, earth colors were used, but they were not very bright. Gradually, people discovered how to make brilliant blues and greens, and the new pigments were traded over long distances. Today, most pigments are synthetic (man-made).

◀ The Lascaux cave paintings are one of only a few surviving examples of prehistoric art.

▶ One word for a deep but bright blue is azure, taken from the pigment azurite.

62 **Pigments need to have a binding agent to hold them in place.** Otherwise, they just turn back to powder after any water has evaporated. One natural binding agent is egg yolk (the yellow part of the egg).

▶ Artists have long prized the intense blue made from the semi-precious stone lapis lazuli.

63 **Chalk was the first substance to be used as white pigment, while earth colors were made with iron minerals.** A copper compound called azurite made a beautiful blue, bettered only by the rarer and more expensive lapis lazuli. The mineral pigment terra verte was used to make green paint, and was so common around Verona, Italy, that it was also known as Verona Green.

▲ Made from a copper compound, green malachite has been in use as a pigment since the Bronze Age in Egypt.

64 **Ancient Egyptian beauties used mineral make-up!** Women of the time used green malachite, along with the black minerals galena or lead sulphide, for eye make-up. Other minerals were used for beauty treatments, and the mineral jasper was used to cure eye infections.

▶ The abundant minerals found or traded by the ancient Egyptians were used for make-up and body decoration.

33

Metal minerals

65 **Most minerals are mixtures known as compounds.** However, there are about 20 "native elements" that rarely mix and are mostly pure. Most of these are metals and without them our world would be very different.

66 **Metals are mined, quarried or dredged up.** At this point, they are known as ore, the word for rock containing metals. The ore is heated beyond its melting point (this is called smelting), and the precious metal is poured out as a liquid and put in a mold to set.

67 **Silver has long featured in jewelry, but it is also used in the electronics industry.** It is found as small specks or thin wiry shapes in igneous rock. Today, silver is less valuable than gold, but in the past it has been rarer than gold, and so more valuable. It goes dull and black very quickly, so it has to be polished to make it shiny.

▲ At a smelting works, metal ore is heated past its melting point and the liquid is poured to set in a mold.

68 Aluminium is quite a common metal—it makes up 8 percent of the weight of the Earth's crust. It is found in about 270 minerals, but is mainly extracted from the ore bauxite. It is light but strong, and is used to make vehicles such as cars and planes as well as many other things. Aluminium isn't magnetic, unlike iron.

▲ ▶ Bauxite ore produces aluminium, a strong but light metal that is ideal for forming the body of vehicles such as planes.

▶ Bronze is the most popular material for metal sculptures. This bronze and marble sculpture is *The Thinker* by Rodin.

69 Metals can be mixed together to make alloys. One of the most important alloys in our history is bronze, a blend of copper and tin. Copper is soft, so wasn't useful for tools or containers, as it didn't stay sharp or in shape. Adding tin made it harder and allowed people to make swords, armor, plows and cooking pots.

▼ With its red-gold color, copper makes one of the most distinctive metals and is found in many minerals.

70 Platinum is one of the rarest metals. It is 30 times more scarce than gold and is usually found as fine grains. Most platinum is found in two parts of the world—Russia and South Africa. It is used in jewelry, laboratories and in catalytic converters (devices used to reduce damaging substances in car emissions). Some coins were made from it in the past.

Buried treasure

◀ Gold panners scoop up the riverbed and shake their pans to see if any pieces of gold are hidden in the rocks and mud.

71 **Gold is one of the most valuable materials.** It has been used as money and as jewelry and decoration for centuries. One of the reasons that it is so precious is that it is very hard to find. Gold is a pure element—it rarely mixes with other minerals.

72 **Gold forms in igneous and sedimentary rocks.** It is sometimes found in lumps known as nuggets, but more commonly as tiny specks. People still pan for gold today, filtering gravel and sand in the hope that they will find some heavier gold grains in their sieve.

TRUE OR FALSE?

1. The mineral pyrite is worth the same as gold.
2. Gold is often used in jewelry.
3. Gold was only recently discovered.

Answers:
1. False 2. True
3. False, it has been used since ancient times

◀ Gold sometimes forms in veins of quartz that are then extracted and smelted.

73 **The ancient Egyptians decorated their temples with gold.** The Turin Papyrus, drawn in 1160 BCE, shows a gold mine in the Egyptian desert. Gold is good to work with since it can be softened and shaped relatively easily. It is also very strong and polishes well.

◀ "Bling" is the slang term for flashy jewelry with lots of gold in it, as worn here by the rapper Slick Rick.

▲ Tutankhamun's death mask was made of solid gold decorated with semi-precious stones and glass. It weighs 22 pounds (10 kilograms).

74 **When lots of people travel to an area where gold has been found, it is called a gold rush.** Gold rushes occurred in Roman times and during the Spanish conquest of the Americas. In the 19th century, whole towns were founded in America, Brazil and Australia when gold-panners moved in and started their search.

75 **Some minerals look like gold.** Known as "fool's gold," pyrite and chalcopyrite have often been mistaken for the real thing because they resemble it so closely. Both are harder than real gold.

▶ Fool's gold can still be useful—it makes sparks when struck and was used in early firearms.

Special effects

76 **A firework display is a big mineral burn-up.** The colors depend on which mineral is used. For example, celestite burns red, while greens are from barite, tourmaline burns yellow and copper burns blue. Firework makers mix minerals into compounds to create new colors. Flashes and shower effects are made with aluminium. The smell from fireworks is actually the mineral sulphur burning.

◀ The blues in a firework display are produced by copper minerals being burnt.

77 **Ultraviolet (UV) light makes some minerals glow fantastic colors that are completely different to their dull appearance in daylight.** This is called fluorescence after the best example, fluorite. This mineral shines blue or green in UV light, probably because it has traces of radioactive uranium.

78 **Gypsum can be dried into a powder.** This powder forms the base for many plasters (such as plaster of Paris) and cements. It is also used in fertilizers and paper.

▲ Fluorite shines in UV light and it also glows when gently heated.

► Coal mining is dangerous because the seams of coal are deep under the ground.

▲ Coal can be treated so that it burns without producing smoke.

79 Fossil fuels such as coal, oil and gas are made from minerals found in the remains of plants that lived millions of years ago. They are used to get energy because they burn well. Coal is solid, and mostly made up of the element carbon.

80 Kaolin is named after Kao-ling hill in China, where it has been quarried for 1,400 years. Made from the mineral kaolinite, it is a soft, white and fine-grained clay used to make porcelain. It has many uses – it is also found in some light bulbs, medicines and glossy paper.

► This kaolin (china clay) mine is in St. Austell, Cornwall, UK.

A mineral meal

Cheese is an excellent source of the mineral apatite

81 **Our bodies need minerals to stay healthy.** The mineral apatite helps to form teeth and bones (its chemical name is calcium phosphate). We get it from dairy foods such as cheese.

82 **We need iron in our blood.** It is found in red meat and eggs. Potassium keeps our muscles working (bananas are full of it). Zinc helps us fight diseases and heal cuts—it is found in meat and beans.

▶ People have mined salt for thousands of years. Salt was once so valuable that Roman soldiers were paid with it.

83 **The most commonly used mineral is salt.** Also known as table salt and rock salt, its chemical name is halite, or sodium chloride. Salt forms where salty water evaporates. Thick layers of it can be found in some sedimentary rock. Some salt is mined underground. Shafts are dug and the salt is loosened with an explosion and then removed.

Eggs are a source of iron

Pulses such as beans provide zinc

Bananas are an excellent source of potassium

▲ The minerals we need to keep our bodies healthy come from the foods we eat. This is one reason why it is so important to eat a varied diet.

84
Your body is like a machine, and it needs minerals to function. In total, about four percent of your body is made up of minerals. This includes small amounts of manganese, copper, iodine, cobalt, fluoride, selenium and many others.

▶ Calcite defines point 3 on the hardness scale. It forms as sharply pointed or flattened six-sided crystals.

85
Plants take minerals from the soil as part of the mix of nutrients they need to live. Minerals used by plants include sulphides, sulphates, calcium and magnesium. They are taken up through the roots.

86
Have you ever noticed the cream-colored "fur" that collects in tea-pots? It is actually a form of calcite, one of the most common minerals in the world. It dissolves in water and then gets left behind. Calcite is the main ingredient in limestone, marble and chalk.

Gems and jewels

87 Gemstones are crystals of natural minerals that shine or sparkle in beautiful colors. They are very popular set in jewelry such as rings, earrings, necklaces and bracelets. They look dull when they are dug up in rocks, but then they are cut to shape and polished to sparkle.

88 The mineral corundum forms blue sapphires and red rubies. These are two of the most precious gemstones. Corundum is very hard (second only to diamonds) and is used to make emery boards that people use to file their nails. It is colorless when pure and is made red by tiny amounts of chromium, or blue by the presence of iron and titanium.

◄ One of the British Crown Jewels, the Imperial State Crown contains diamonds, pearls, sapphires, emeralds and rubies.

I DON'T BELIEVE IT!

Gems are given a carat rating, which refers to their weight (a carat is about one-fifth of a gram). The word carat comes from the ancient Greek practice of weighing gems using carob tree seeds.

▼ Ruby is regarded as the king of gemstones because of its rich red coloring and its strength.

▶ Everybody has a birthstone and some people like to wear their own special gem.

91

One of the earliest highly prized gems was emerald. The Egyptians sent slaves to work in the desert mining these green gems. The Inca of South America regarded them as sacred and decorated their golden statues and jewelry with them.

89

Some gemstones are identified with certain months. For example, May is emerald and October is opal. There are even meanings given to gemstones, such as peace for amethyst and energy for topaz.

90

There are 130 different gemstones, of which the rarest are diamonds, emeralds, rubies and sapphires. Dealers describe gemstones using the four Cs: clarity, color, cut and carat (weight). The largest stones are usually the most valuable.

January Garnet

February Amethyst

March Aquamarine

April Diamond

May Emerald

June Pearl

July Ruby

August Peridot

September Sapphire

October Opal

November Topaz

December Turquoise

Diamonds are forever

◀ Large machinery is used to uncover diamond-rich gravel at this coastal diamond mine in Namibia, Africa.

92 **Diamonds are the hardest known mineral.** They are named after the Greek word for indestructible, *adamas*. They are the toughest known material, scoring 10 on the mineral hardness scale. They are used in jewelry, and also in industry, for cutting and drilling through dense materials such as rock.

93 **Most diamonds are mined from a rock called kimberlite.** They form deep in the Earth, up to 125 miles (200 kilometers) below the surface, under high pressure and at temperatures between 1650° and 2370° F (900° and 1300° C). Some diamond mine tunnels have to be cooled for people to work in because they are heated by the Earth's magma.

◀ The Millennium Star diamond is one of the most famous in the world. It took three years to cut it into this perfect pear shape using lasers.

◀ This diamond-bearing rock formed deep in the Earth and was brought up by an erupting volcano.

▶ This 18th-century skull is studded with 8,601 diamonds to create a piece of art that has been valued at $76.5 million.

94

When they are cut and polished, diamonds sparkle beautifully. This makes them very popular for jewelry, but it wasn't until the Middle Ages that jewelers cut and polished diamonds and discovered their amazing brilliance.

95

If diamonds are heated above 1652° F (900° C), they become graphite, the mineral that is mixed with clay to form the "lead" in pencils. It gets its name from the Greek word for writing, *graphein*. Graphite is a soft and very stable mineral, and it is used for lots of things, from tennis rackets to steel making and nuclear power stations.

▶ Diamonds mean glamour, so movie stars such as Elizabeth Taylor (shown here at the 42nd Annual Academy Awards in 1970) spend huge amounts of money on them.

How to be a geologist

96 Geology is the study of the Earth, including its rocks and minerals. Some people do it as a hobby, others as a job. Geologists might be called in to help plan where to build roads and houses or to look for precious gems or minerals. Many are employed helping to search for valuable resources such as metals, gas and oil.

▼ Geologists study how rocks form and measure how much they move as the Earth changes.

STUDYING ROCKS

Study a piece of rock through a magnifing glass. How many colors can you find? You might find it's made of tiny grains with shiny surfaces—crystals. Try to find any tiny dark flecks of mica, or glassy grains of quartz. Look for evidence of sea creatures—you might be looking at the fossil of something that swam in the oceans millions of years ago.

97 If you want to collect rocks, fossils and minerals you must have permission from the landowner and go with an adult. You need a notebook, map, guidebook, magnifing glass, gloves, boots and maybe a helmet. Bring a digital camera to take pictures of what you find.

98 **Don't collect from cliffs and quarry walls, as they can be dangerous.** Only use a hammer if you've been shown how. You can just collect information, noted down or photographed. Wrap any specimens in newspaper or other material to stop them getting damaged.

99 **Beaches are great places to hunt for rocks and fossils.** Fossils can be exposed as the wind and waves wash away soil and loose rock. You could start by studying pebbles. Different colors probably indicate different minerals. Some rocks may have been in the same place for centuries, others could have come in on the tide that day. You can also look at the rock strata of cliffs.

▲ A geologist picks up a piece of molten rock from a lava flow. The study of volcanoes is called volcanology.

24

100 **Geology really started about 250 years ago with James Hutton (1726–97).** Hutton showed that rivers wash away rocks and even eventually whole hills and mountains. He also noticed that rocks were formed from crystals and could be changed by the Earth's heat. He was one of the first people to show that our planet was far older than had been thought. We now know it is about 4.6 billion years old and has been through many stages and changes.

◄ In Hutton's time many people believed that all rocks formed in the sea. His idea that they came from deep in the Earth was thought very strange at first.

Index

Entries in **bold** refer to main subject entries. Entries in *italics* refer to illustrations.